E MILY
D ICKINSON

$ON\ LOVE$

$\mathcal{E}$MILY $\mathcal{D}$ICKINSON

$O\mathcal{N}$ $LO\mathcal{V}\mathcal{E}$

BARNES
&NOBLE
BOOKS
NEW YORK

This edition published by Barnes & Noble, Inc.

1993 Barnes & Noble Books

Book design by Charles Ziga, Ziga Design

ISBN 1-56619-192-0

Printed and bound in the United States of America

M 9 8 7 6 5 4 3

CONTENTS

INTRODUCTION

Contrary to her image as a timid and forbearing woman, Emily Dickinson's love poems speak of love from a perspective both knowing and blissful. Yet because of her renowned reclusive life, the strength and nobility which kindles her poetry has largely been overlooked, and many initiates of her work take her seclusion as a sign of cowardliness. They disregard the courage and conviction necessary to produce a poetry as vital and important as hers. For only an insightful, visionary poet could create these poems that inspire and inform our sense of the contrary aspects within love with an immediacy sympathetic to our own modern sensibilities. A few scholars, in fact, have claimed that in the future Emily Dickinson and Walt Whitman will be considered America's most seminal poets.

If our reading of Emily Dickinson is unnecessarily clouded today by certain aspects of her personal life, it is a mist of legends and myths whose beginnings formed during her own lifetime.

By the time of her late thirties, the townspeople of Amherst were already gossiping about this women who would not leave her home for periods of time lasting years. Even then, they called her the "Myth," and the early legends surrounding her were those of a poet whose work

VII

resulted from the frustrations of living with an over-tyrannical father, inhabiting a dysfunctional home, or a lover's tryst turned tragic. And today, though a number of meticulous, well-researched studies have been written about her life and work since then, something of these infamous legends still clings to her.

Emily Dickinson was born in 1830, the second of three children, and grew up in the last years of a truly Puritanical America still very wary of writings such as Emerson's or Shakespeare's that would "joggle the mind." Much of her early legend has its roots in her supposedly "ogre father," Edward Dickinson, who was a powerful leader in Amherst, and U.S. Representative for one term. But such a high public profile in politics, accompanied by its demanding schedule, could have hardly allowed him the time to be the stern disciplinarian the early legends made him out to be. Emily Dickinson, in fact, admired her father greatly for his astuteness in handling his public life and his death affected her as one of the toughest emotional experiences that she would ever have to overcome.

It is doubtful the single cause for Emily Dickinson's seclusion will ever be truly discovered. It is more likely, however, that her self-imposed isolation was the culmination of a long process resulting from the early loss of close friends, the dislike of her contemporary world, her family's financial stability, and her strong conviction in herself as a poet.

Emily Dickinson's early fascination with poetry and her desire to be a poet slowly drew her away from many of the young people she had been friends with in her teens. As she grew into her mid-twenties, she became increasingly interested in expressing herself in a metaphorical language that could best be deciphered with only a poet's sensibility. The poetic metaphor no doubt helped her achieve that "brimful" feeling she continually sought to experience in life, but the poetic metaphor can also be something of a lethal sword in opening worlds of both enthusiasm and despair. When moving the reader from one place to an "other" or "elsewhere," the metaphor inspires an enthusiasm in the reader when this "other" is discovered as something having its correspondence to actual life. But, when this otherness is found wanting, as in Emily Dickinson's poem, "I envy seas whereon he rides," her fear of a "noon of an eternal night" reveals both the importance she places on the metaphor and the despair behind her fear of its absence.

Unable to find her passion for anything in her immediate surroundings, and spending more time taking care of her bedridden mother, it is not difficult to see why her Amherst home became so important to her and the metaphor of the House so prominent in her poetry. For Emily Dickinson, her home was "a holy thing," a place wherein she could discover both a metaphor for nature, "the House not made with Hands," and for life itself, "We outgrow love like other things/And put it in the drawer." So, contrary to the earlier legends of her repressive domestic life, it is very plausible that one of the reasons for her seclusion was the rich life she discovered there. It is estimated by later editors of her work that in 1862 she wrote an incredible number of poems totaling over 350 pieces. Even from her darkest perspective, she still saw her house as something of a "magic prison."

Her cloistered life though, also greatly influenced the subject of her poems. Her dedication to her work and her solitude are marked by a deep absence of the beloved in her love poems. The poems collected here dwell on the many aspects of love, but there is always the sense that the other to whom many of the poems are addressed is distant—as often were the men she was enamored with.

To whom were her love poems addressed? The two men—the preacher Charles Wadsworth, and the editor Samuel Bowles—with whom Emily Dickinson involved herself (sometime between 1855 and 1863) were both married, successful, and very occupied with their careers. She sought their attention through letters and they corresponded in return and visited her home periodically, but they never truly returned her affections.

Richard Sewell, in his *The Life of Emily Dickinson,* states that most of her love poems were directed to Samuel Bowles, the extremely busy editor of the daily *Springfield Republican,* who led an outgoing, worldly lifestyle — the exact opposite of Emily Dickinson's reflective life at home. Yet, her attraction to him was strong. As she saw herself advancing and mastering her art, it is very possible that she looked up to him not only as someone to provide emotional comfort, but also to help her get her poems published. She had sent him a few poems, but he showed no special appreciation or deep understanding towards them at all. As she came to realize that she would never find happiness with him, her sense of despair only deepened.

This absence or silence between her and the men she sought out plays an active role in her poetry. In a number of these love poems there is a dialogue between the heart/body and the soul, with a majority of the poems taking up the voice of the soul. This is a very telling aspect of her love poems, and it reveals why a visionary, domestic poet would find such a strong attraction to worldly men of affairs (who in turn held some slight interest in her). Emily Dickinson's relationship to these men mirrors closely the contrary elements of her poetry which she struggled with to bring into the rhythms of her work. The distance from which she conducted her relationships heightened the importance and intensity of the "other," the poetic metaphor in her work. It created a bridge across two opposing cliffs from which she could see the causes for separation and unity in her relationships. And this distance also taught her self-reliance: "Love is its own rescue, for we — at our Supremest, are but its trembling Emblems."

These love poems are the result of an extremely noble love, where the attractions of the world are recognized and embraced and infused with a love both lasting and golden. And this, too, is in keeping with Emily Dickinson's life: her focus on her family's large Amherst house as a sacred place and her conviction to keep her "golden thread" perspective on life — seeing only those things and people that she felt would give her work its most lasting quality. This approach toward an enduring love kept her experience to love open as she advanced in years. For, after her earlier disappointments, she finally experienced in her late years with Otis Phillips Lord, a successful lawyer and politician, the love between herself and another that had never before been fulfilled.

— ROBERT YAGLEY
1993

EMILY DICKINSON

ON LOVE

*I*t's all I have to bring to-day,
  This, and my heart beside,
This, and my heart, and all the fields,
  And all the meadows wide.
Be sure you count, should I forget,—
  Some one the sun could tell,—
This, and my heart, and all the bees
  Which in the clover dwell.

*M*ine by the right of the white election!
Mine by the royal seal!
Mine by the sign in the scarlet prison
Bars cannot conceal!

Mine, here in vision and in veto!
Mine, by the grave's repeal!
Titled, confirmed,— delirious charter!
Mine, while the ages steal!

❧❧ II ❧❧

*Y*ou left me, sweet, two legacies,—
A legacy of love
A Heavenly Father would content,
Had He the offer of;

You left me boundaries of pain
Capacious as the sea,
Between eternity and time,
Your consciousness and me.

*A*lter? When the hills do.
Falter? When the sun
Question if his glory
Be the perfect one.

Surfeit? When the daffodil
Doth of the dew:
Even as herself, O friend!
I will of you!

*E*lysium is as far as to
The very nearest room,
If in that room a friend await
Felicity or doom.

What fortitude the soul contains,
That it can so endure
The accent of a coming foot,
The opening of a door!

❧ V ❧

*D*oubt me, my dim companion!
Why, God would be content
With but a fraction of the love
Poured thee without a stint.
The whole of me, forever,
What more the woman can,—
Say quick, that I may dower thee
With last delight I own!

It cannot be my spirit,
For that was thine before;
I ceded all of dust I knew,—
What opulence the more
Had I, a humble maiden,
Whose farthest of degree
Was that she might
Some distant heaven,
Dwell timidly with thee!

*I*f you were coming in the fall,
I'd brush the summer by
With half a smile and half a spurn,
As housewives do a fly.

If I could see you in a year,
I'd wind the months in balls,
And put them each in separate drawers,
Until their time befalls.

If only centuries delayed,
I'd count them on my hand,
Subtracting till my fingers dropped
Into Van Diemen's land.

If certain, when this life was out,
That yours and mine should be,
I'd toss it yonder like a rind,
And taste eternity.

But now, all ignorant of the length
Of time's uncertain wing,
It goads me, like the goblin bee,
That will not state its sting.

 ∽ **VII** ∽

I hide myself within my flower,
That wearing on your breast,
You, unsuspecting, wear me too—
And angels know the rest.

I hide myself within my flower,
That, fading from your vase,
You, unsuspecting, feel for me
Almost a loneliness.

❦ VIII ❦

*T*hat I did always love,
I bring thee proof:
That till I loved
I did not love enough.

That I shall love alway,
I offer thee
That love is life,
And life hath immortality.

This, dost thou doubt, sweet?
Then have I
Nothing to show
But Calvary.

*H*ave you got a brook in your little heart,
Where bashful flowers blow,
And blushing birds go down to drink,
And shadows tremble so?

And nobody knows, so still it flows,
That any brook is there;
And yet your little draught of life
Is daily drunken there.

Then look out for the little brook in March,
When the rivers overflow,
And the snows come hurrying from the hills,
And the bridges often go.

And later, in August it may be,
When the meadows parching lie,
Beware, lest this little brook of life
Some burning noon go dry!

❧ X ❧

*A*s if some little Arctic flower,
Upon the polar hem,
Went wandering down the latitudes,
Until it puzzled came
To continents of summer,
To firmaments of sun,
To strange, bright crowds of flowers,
And birds of foreign tongue!
I say, as if this little flower
To Eden wandered in—
What then? Why, nothing, only
Your inference therefrom!

❦ XI ❦

*M*y river runs to thee:
Blue sea, wilt welcome me?

My river waits reply.
Oh sea, look graciously!

I'll fetch thee brooks
From spotted nooks,—

Say, sea,
Take me!

I cannot live with you,
It would be life,
And life is over there
Behind the shelf

The sexton keeps the key to,
Putting up
Our life, his porcelain,
Like a cup

Discarded of the housewife,
Quaint or broken;
A newer Sèvres pleases,
Old ones crack.

I could not die with you,
For one must wait
To shut the other's gaze down,—
You could not.

And I, could I stand by
And see you freeze,
Without my right of frost,
Death's privilege?

Nor could I rise with you,
Because your face
Would put out Jesus',
That new grace

Glow plain and foreign
On my homesick eye,
Except that you, than he
Shone closer by.

They'd judge us—how?
For you served heaven, you know,
Or sought to;
I could not,

Because you saturated sight,
And I had no more eyes
For sordid excellence
As Paradise.

And were you lost, I would be,
Though my name
Rang loudest
On the heavenly fame.

And were you saved,
And I condemned to be
Where you were not,
That self were hell to me.

So we must keep apart,
You there, I here,
With just the door ajar
That oceans are,
And prayer,
And that pale sustenance,
Despair!

∾ XIII ∾

*T*here came a day at summer's full
Entirely for me;
I thought that such were for the saints,
Where revelations be.

The sun, as common, went abroad,
The flowers, accustomed, blew,
As if no sail the solstice passed
That maketh all things new.

The time was scarce profaned by speech;
The symbol of a word
Was needless, as at sacrament
The wardrobe of our Lord.

Each was to each the sealed church,
Permitted to commune this time,
Lest we too awkward show
At supper of the Lamb.

The hours slid fast, as hours will,
Clutched tight by greedy hands;
So faces on two decks look back,
Bound to opposing lands.

And so, when all the time had failed,
Without external sound,
Each bound the other's crucifix,
We gave no other bond.

Sufficient troth that we shall rise—
Deposed, at length, the grave—
To that new marriage, justified
Through Calvaries of Love!

❧ XIV ❧

*T*was a long parting, but the time
For interview had come;
Before the judgment-seat of God,
The last and second time

These fleshless lovers met,
A heaven in a gaze,
A heaven of heavens, the privilege
Of one another's eyes.

No lifetime set on them,
Apparelled as the new
Unborn, except they had beheld,
Born everlasting now.

Was bridal e'er like this?
A paradise, the host,
And cherubim and seraphim
The most familiar guest.

I'm wife; I've finished that,
That other state;
I'm Czar, I'm woman now:
It's safer so.

How odd the girl's life looks
Behind this soft eclipse!
I think that earth seems so
To those in heaven now.

This being comfort, then
That other kind was pain;
But why compare?
I'm wife! stop there!

*S*he rose to his requirement, dropped
The playthings of her life
To take the honorable work
Of woman and of wife.

If aught she missed in her new day
Of amplitude, or awe,
Or first prospective, or the gold
In using wore away,

It lay unmentioned, as the sea
Develops pearl and weed,
But only to himself is known
The fathoms they abide.

∽ XVII ∽

*C*ome slowly, Eden!
Lips unused to thee,
Bashful, sip thy jasmines,
As the fainting bee,

Reaching late his flower,
Round her chamber hums,
Counts his nectars — enters,
And is lost in balms!

XVIII

*O*f all the souls that stand create
I have elected one.
When sense from spirit files away,
And subterfuge is done;

When that which is and that which was
Apart, intrinsic, stand,
And this brief tragedy of flesh
Is shifted like a sand;

When figures show their royal front
And mists are carved away,—
Behold the atom I preferred
To all the lists of clay!

❧ XIX ❧

I have no life but this,
To lead it here;
Nor any death, but lest
Dispelled from there;

Nor tie to earths to come,
Nor action new,
Except through this extent,
The realm of you.

Your riches taught me poverty.
Myself a millionaire
In little wealths,—as girls could boast,—
Till broad as Buenos Ayre,

You drifted your dominions
A different Peru;
And I esteemed all poverty,
For life's estate with you.

Of mines I little know, myself,
But just the names of gems,—
The colors of the commonest;
And scarce of diadems

So much that, did I meet the queen,
Her glory I should know:
But this must be a different wealth,
To miss it beggars so.

I'm sure 't is India all day
To those who look on you
Without a stint, without a blame,—
Might I but be the Jew!

I'm sure it is Golconda,
Beyond my power to deem,—
To have a smile for mine each day,
How better than a gem!

At least, it solaces to know
That there exists a gold,
Although I prove it just in time
Its distance to behold!

It's far, far treasure to surmise,
and estimate the pearl
That slipped my simple fingers through
While just a girl at school!

I gave myself to him,
And took himself for pay.
The solemn contract of a life
Was ratified this way.

The wealth might disappoint,
Myself a poorer prove
Than this great purchaser suspect,
The daily own of Love

Depreciate the vision;
But, till the merchant buy,
Still fable, in the isles of spice,
The subtle cargoes lie.

At least, 't is mutual risk,—
Some found it mutual gain;
Sweet debt of Life,—each night to owe,
Insolvent, every noon.

Going to him! Happy letter! Tell him—
Tell him the page I did n't write;
Tell him I only said the syntax,
And left the verb and the pronoun out.
Tell him just how the fingers hurried,
Then how they waded, slow, slow, slow;
And then you wished you had eyes in your pages,
So you could see what moved them so.

"Tell him it wasn't a practised writer,
You guessed, from the way the sentence toiled;
You could hear the bodice tug, behind you,
As if it held but the might of a child;
You almost pitied it, you, it worked so.
Tell him—No, you may quibble there,
For it would split his heart to know it,
And then you and I were silenter.

"Tell him night finished before we finished,
And the old clock kept neighing 'day!'
And you got sleepy and begged to be ended—
What could it hinder so, to say?
Tell him just how she sealed you, cautious,
But if he ask where you are hid
Until to-morrow,—happy letter!
Gesture, coquette, and shake your head!"

*T*he way I read a letter's this:
'T is first I lock the door,
And push it with my fingers next,
For transport it be sure.

And then I go the furthest off
To counteract a knock;
Then draw my little letter forth
And softly pick its lock.

Then, glancing narrow at the wall,
And narrow at the floor,
For firm conviction of a mouse
Not exorcised before,

Peruse how infinite I am
To—no one that you know!
And sigh for lack of heaven,—but not
The heaven the creeds bestow.

❦ XXIV ❦

Wild nights! Wild nights!
Were I with thee,
Wild nights should be
Our luxury!

Futile the winds
To a heart in port,—
Done with the compass,
Done with the chart.

Rowing in Eden!
Ah! the sea!
Might I but moor
To-night in thee!

❧ XXV ❧

*D*id the harebell loose her girdle
To the lover bee,
Would the bee the harebell hallow
Much as formerly?

Did the paradise, persuaded,
Yield her moat of pearl,
Would the Eden be an Eden,
Or the earl an carl?

❧ XXVI ❧

A charm invests a face
Imperfectly beheld,—
The lady dare not lift her veil
For fear it be dispelled.

But peers beyond her mesh,
And wishes, and denies,—
Lest interview annul a want
That image satisfies.

☙ XXVII ☙

*T*he rose did caper on her cheek,
Her bodice rose and fell,
Her pretty speech, like drunken men,
Did stagger pitiful.

Her fingers fumbled at her work,—
Her needle would not go;
What ailed so smart a little maid
It puzzled me to know,

Till opposite I spied a cheek
That bore another rose;
Just opposite, another speech
That like the drunkard goes;

A vest that, like the bodice, danced
To the immortal tune,—
Till those two troubled little clocks
Ticked softly into one.

∾ XXVIII ∾

In lands I never saw, they say,
Immortal Alps look down,
Whose bonnets touch the firmament,
Whose sandals touch the town,—

Meek at whose everlasting feet
A myriad daisies play.
Which, sir, are you, and which am I,
Upon an August day?

⁓ XXIX ⁓

*T*he moon is distant from the sea,
And yet with amber hands
She leads him, docile as a boy,
Along appointed sands.

He never misses a degree;
Obedient to her eye,
He comes just so far toward the town,
Just so far goes away.

Oh, Signor, thine the amber hand,
And mine the distant sea,—
Obedient to the least command
Thine eyes impose on me.

He put the belt around my life,—
I heard the buckle snap,
And turned away, imperial,
My lifetime folding up
Deliberate, as a duke would do
A kingdom's title-deed,—
Henceforth a dedicated sort,
A member of the cloud.

Yet not too far to come at call,
And do the little toils
That make the circuit of the rest,
And deal occasional smiles
To lives that stoop to notice mine
And kindly ask it in,—
Whose invitation, knew you not
For whom I must decline?

❦ XXXI ❦

*W*hat if I say I shall not wait?
What if I burst the fleshly gate
And pass, escaped, to thee?
What if I file this mortal off,
See where it hurt me,—that's enough,—
And wade in liberty?

They cannot take us any more,—
Dungeons may call, and guns implore;
Unmeaning now, to me,
As laughter was an hour ago,
Or laces, or a travelling show,
Or who died yesterday!

XXXII

*P*roud of my broken heart since thou didst break it,
   Proud of the pain I did not feel till thee,
Proud of my night since thou with moons dost slake it,
   Not to partake thy passion, my humility.

*M*y worthiness is all my doubt,
  His merit all my fear,
Contrasting which, my qualities
  Do lowlier appear;

Lest I should insufficient prove
  For his beloved need,
The chiefest apprehension
  Within my loving creed.

So I, the undivine abode
  Of his elect content,
Conform my soul as 't were a church
  Unto her sacrament.

*L*ove is anterior to life,
   Posterior to death,
Initial of creation, and
   The exponent of breath.

❧ XXXV ❧

*W*hen roses cease to bloom, dear,
  And violets are done,
When bumble-bees in solemn flight
  Have passed beyond the sun,

The hand that paused to gather
  Upon this summer's day
Will idle lie, in Auburn,—
  Then take my flower, pray!

XXXVI

*S*ummer for thee grant I may be
  When summer days are flown!
Thy music still when whippoorwill
  And oriole are done!

For thee to bloom, I'll skip the tomb
  And sow my blossoms o'er!
Pray gather me, Anemone,
  Thy flower forevermore!

*T*o lose thee, sweeter than to gain
   All other hearts I knew.
'T is true the drought is destitute,
   But then I had the dew!

The Caspian has its realms of sand,
   Its other realm of sea;
Without the sterile perquisite
   No Caspian could be.

❧ XXXVIII ❧

*P*oor little heart!
  Did they forget thee?
Then dinna care! Then dinna care!

  Proud little heart!
  Did they forsake thee?
Be debonair! Be debonair!

  Frail little heart!
  I would not break thee:
Could'st credit me? Could'st credit me?

  Gay little heart!
  Like morning glory
Thou'll wilted be; thou'll wilted be!

ᐁᐁ XXXIX ᐁᐁ

I've got an arrow here;
  Loving the hand that sent it,
I the dart revere.

Fell, they will say, in "skirmish"!
  Vanquished, my soul will know,
By but a simple arrow
  Sped by an archer's bow.

❦ XL ❦

*H*e fumbles at your spirit
   As players at the keys
Before they drop full music on;
   He stuns you by degrees,

Prepares your brittle substance
   For the ethereal blow,
By fainter hammers, further heard,
   Then nearer, then so slow

Your breath has time to straighten,
   Your brain to bubble cool,—
Deals one imperial thunderbolt
   That scalps your naked soul.

❧❧ XLI ❧❧

*H*eart, we will forget him!
   You and I, to-night!
You may forget the warmth he gave,
   I will forget the light.

When you have done, pray tell me,
   That I my thoughts may dim;
Haste! lest while you're lagging,
   I may remember him!

❦ XLII ❦

*W*e outgrow love like other things
　　And put it in the drawer,
Till it an antique fashion shows
　　Like costumes grandsires wore.

⇜ XLIII ⇝

Not with a club the heart is broken,
  Nor with a stone;
A whip, so small you could not see it,
  I've known

To lash the magic creature
  Till it fell,
Yet that whip's name too noblc
  Then to tell.

Magnanimous of bird
  By boy descried,
To sing unto the stone
  Of which it died.

My friend must be a bird,
　　Because it flies!
Mortal my friend must be,
　　Because it dies!
Barbs has it, like a bee.
Ah, curious friend,
　　Thou puzzlest me!

⇝ XLV ⇝

*H*e touched me, so I live to know
That such a day, permitted so,
    I groped upon his breast.
It was a boundless place to me,
And silenced, as the awful sea
    Puts minor streams to rest.

And now, I'm different from before,
As if I breathed superior air,
    Or brushed a royal gown;
My feet, too, that had wandered so,
My gypsy face transfigured now
    To tenderer renown.

❧ XLVI ❧

I live with him, I see his face;
　　I go no more away
For visitor, or sundown;
　　Death's single privacy,

The only one forestalling mine,
　　And that by right that he
Presents a claim invisible,
　　No wedlock granted me.

I live with him, I hear his voice,
　　I stand alive to-day
To witness to the certainty
　　Of immortality

Taught me by Time,—the lower way,
　　Conviction every day,—
That life like this is endless,
　　Be judgment what it may.

❦ XLVII ❦

I envy seas whereon he rides,
   I envy spokes of wheels
Of chariots that him convey,
   I envy speechless hills

That gaze upon his journey;
   How easy all can see
What is forbidden utterly
   As heaven, unto me!

I envy nests of sparrows
   That dot his distant eaves,
The wealthy fly upon his pane,
   The happy, happy leaves

That just abroad his window
   Have summer's leave to be,
The earrings of Pizarro
   Could not obtain for me.

I envy light that wakes him,
    And bells that boldly ring
To tell him it is noon abroad,—
    Myself his noon could bring,

Yet interdict my blossom
    And abrogate my bee,
Lest noon in everlasting night
    Drop Gabriel and me.

❧ XLVIII ❧

*T*itle divine is mine
The Wife without
The Sign.
Acute degree
Conferred on me—
Empress of Calvary.
Royal all but the
Crown—
Betrothed, without the swoon
God gives us women
When two hold
Garnet to garnet,
Gold to gold—
Born—Bridalled—
Shrouded—
In a day
Tri-Victory—
    "My Husband"
Women say
Stroking the melody,
Is this the way?

❧ XLIX ❧

Our share of night to bear,
Our share of morning,
Our blank in bliss to fill,
Our blank in scorning.

Here a star, and there a star,
Some lose their way.
Here a mist, and there a mist,
Afterwards — day!

*F*or each ecstatic instant
We must an anguish pay
In keen and quivering ratio
To the ecstasy.

For each beloved hour
Sharp pittances of years,
Bitter contested farthings
And coffers heaped with tears.

∽∽ LI ∽∽

*V*ictory comes late
And is held low to freezing lips
Too rapt with frost
To take it.
How sweet it would have tasted,
Just a drop!
Was God so economical?
His table's spread too high for us
Unless we dine on tip-toe.
Crumbs fit such little mouths,
Cherries suit robins;
The eagle's golden breakfast
Strangles them.
God keeps his oath to sparrows,
Who of little love
Know how to starve!

*H*eart not so heavy as mine,
Wending late home,
As it passed my window
Whistled itself a tune,—

A careless snatch, a ballad,
A ditty of the street;
Yct to my irritated ear
An anodyne so sweet,

It was as if a bobolink,
Sauntering this way,
Carolled and mused and carolled,
Then bubbled slow away.

It was as if a chirping brook
Upon a toilsome way
Set bleeding feet to minuets
Without the knowing why.

To-morrow, night will come again,
Weary, perhaps, and sore.
Ah, bugle, by my window,
I pray you stroll once more!

∾ LIII ∾

*I*t's such a little thing to weep,
   So short a thing to sigh;
And yet by trades the size of these
   We men and women die!

*M*y life closed twice before its close;
    It yet remains to see
If immortality unveil
    A third even to me,

So huge, so hopeless to conceive,
    As these that twice befell.
Parting is all we know of heaven,
    And all we need of hell.

*W*ho has not found the heaven below
Will fail of it above.
God's residence is next to mine,
His furniture is love.

⋙ LVI ⋘

*F*rom all the jails the boys and girls
    Ecstatically leap,—
Beloved, only afternoon
    That prison does n't keep.

They storm the earth and stun the air,
    A mob of solid bliss.
Alas! that frowns could lie in wait
    For such a foe as this!

❧ LVII ❧

*F*ate slew him, but he did not drop;
  She felled—he did not fall—
Impaled him on her fiercest stakes—
  He neutralized them all.

She stung him, sapped his firm advance,
  But, when her worst was done,
And he, unmoved, regarded her,
  Acknowledged him a man.

❦ LVIII ❦

Who never wanted,—maddest joy
    Remains to him unknown;
The banquet of abstemiousness
    Surpasses that of wine.

Within its hope, though yet ungrasped
    Desire's perfect goal,
No nearer, lest reality
    Should disenthrall thy soul.

❧ LIX ❧

Nature rarer uses yellow
  Than another hue;
Saves she all of that for sunsets,—
  Prodigal of blue,

Spending scarlet like a woman,
  Yellow she affords
Only scantly and selectly,
  Like a lover's words.

❧ LX ❧

*T*wo swimmers wrestled on the spar
Until the morning sun,
When one turned smiling to the land.
O God, the other one!

The stray ships passing spied a face
Upon the waters borne,
With eyes in death still begging raised,
And hands beseeching thrown.

❧❧ LXI ❧❧

*T*he daisy follows soft the sun,
And when his golden walk is done,
   Sits shyly at his feet.
He, waking, finds the flower near.
"Wherefore, marauder, art thou here?"
   "Because, sir, love is sweet!"

We are the flower, Thou the sun!
Forgive us, if as days decline,
   We nearer steal to Thee,—
Enamoured of the parting west,
The peace, the flight, the amethyst,
   Night's possibility!

❦ LXII ❦

*I*f I should die,
And you should live,
And time should gurgle on,
And morn should beam,
And noon should burn,
As it has usual done;
If birds should build as early,
And bees as bustling go,—
One might depart at option
From enterprise below!
'T is sweet to know that stocks will stand
When we with daisies lie,
That commerce will continue,
And trades as briskly fly.
It makes the parting tranquil
And keeps the soul serene,
That gentlemen so sprightly
Conduct the pleasing scene!

❧ LXIII ❧

*W*e cover thee, sweet face.
  Not that we tire of thee,
But that thyself fatigue of us;
  Remember, as thou flee,
We follow thee until
  Thou notice us no more,
And then, reluctant, turn away
  To con thee o'er and o'er,
And blame the scanty love
  We were content to show,
Augmented, sweet, a hundred fold
  If thou would'st take it now.

*T*hat is solemn we have ended,—
　　Be it but a play,
Or a glee among the garrets,
　　Or a holiday,

Or a leaving home; or later,
　　Parting with a world
We have understood, for better
　　Still it be unfurled.

❦ LXV ❦

*G*iven in marriage unto thee,
   Oh, thou celestial host!
Bride of the Father and the Son,
   Bride of the Holy Ghost!

Other betrothal shall dissolve,
   Wedlock of will decay;
Only the keeper of this seal
   Conquers mortality.

❦ LXVI ❧

If I may have it when it's dead
  I will contented be;
If just as soon as breath is out
  It shall belong to me,

Until they lock it in the grave,
  'T is bliss I cannot weigh,
For though they lock thee in the grave,
  Myself can hold the key.

Think of it, lover! I and thee
  Permitted face to face to be;
After a life, a death we'll say,—
  For death was that, and this is thee.

❦ LXVII ❦

I did not reach thee,
But my feet slip nearer every day;
Three Rivers and a Hill to cross,
One Desert and a Sea—
I shall not count the journey one
When I am telling thee.

Two deserts—but the year is cold
So that will help the sand—
One desert crossed, the second one
Will feel as cool as land.
Sahara is too little price
To pay for thy Right hand!

The sea comes last. Step merry, feet!
So short have we to go
To play together we are prone,
But we must labor now,
The last shall be the lightest load
That we have had to draw.

The Sun goes crooked—that is night—
Before he make the bend
We must have passed the middle sea,
Almost we wish the end
Were further off—too great it seems
So near the Whole to stand.

We step like plush, we stand like snow—
The waters murmur now,
Three rivers and the hill are passed,
Two deserts and the sea!
Now Death usurps my premium
And gets the look at Thee.

∼ LXVIII ∼

I'm ceded, I've stopped being theirs;
The name, they dropped upon my face
With water, in the country church,
Is finished using now,
And they can put it with my dolls,
My childhood, and the string of spools
I've finished threading too.

Baptized before without the choice,
But this time consciously, of grace
Unto supremest name,
Called to my full, the crescent dropped,
Existence's whole arc filled up
With one small diadem.

My second rank, too small the first,
Crowned, crowing on my father's breast,
A half unconscious queen;
But this time, adequate, erect,
With will to choose or to reject,
And I choose—just a throne.

LXIX

I held a jewel in my fingers
And went to sleep.
The day was warm, and winds were prosy;
I said: "'T will keep."

I woke and chid my honest fingers,—
The gem was gone;
And now an amethyst remembrance
Is all I own.

Index of First Lines